WANDERLUST

San Francisco

A Creative Guide to the City

BETSY BEIER

WEST
MARGIN
PRESS

SAN FRANCISCO

ALCATRAZ

FISHERMAN'S WHARF

GOLDEN GATE PARK

68

64

HAIGHT-ASHBURY

JAPANTOWN

THE CASTRO

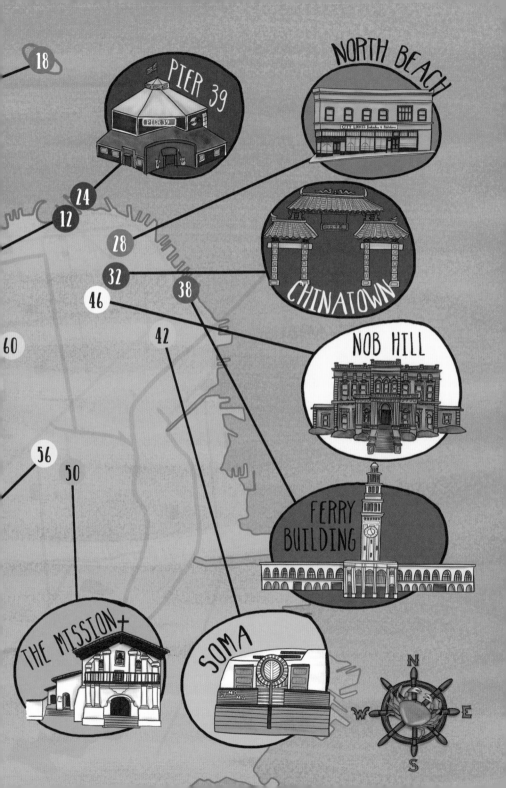

18

PIER 39

NORTH BEACH

24

12

28

32

46

38

CHINATOWN

42

60

NOB HILL

56

50

FERRY BUILDING

THE MISSION

SOMA

N
W E
S

INTRODUCTION

No matter where I am in the world, whenever I tell people I'm from San Francisco, I always get nods of approval. "Oh, San Francisco," they sigh, "what a beautiful city. I would love to go!"

San Francisco is truly a world-class city. It checks off all the traditional boxes—top-notch museums, incredible food, abundant cultural attractions, one-of-a-kind scenery, a thriving economy—yet also retains its West Coast, laid-back personality. There is so much to explore and experience, so let this book serve as a jumping-off point— San Francisco has even more to offer!

I'm a huge believer in experiential travel. When I visit a new location, I like to slow down long enough to be able to capture a sliver of what life might be like to live there. Of course I'll go see the top destinations a city might have to offer, but for me it's about making time to sit at a local cafe for an afternoon and soak up the vibe, or exploring a lesser-known neighborhood and watching people going about their day. It might be simply capturing the colors I see around the place, or making note of the slang words I hear from the locals in conversation.

Experiential travel is also about context, opening your eyes to learn a little about the history of the place while removing any preconceived judgments. Ultimately, it's about being open to any experience that may come your way.

So join me on this creative journey as we explore the incredible city of San Francisco!

GETTING STARTED

Grab a pen, a few color pencils, your phone, and this book, and you are set to go! Use this book to:

EXPLORE THE SIGHTS This book can be used as a travel guide before you head off on your journey or while you are actually at a location and looking around. Most chapters are about a specific neighborhood and some are citywide. Within each chapter, there is some high-level history, plus interesting facts and stories to give you a taste of the area. Just use the map on page 2 to look up the destination you are interested in exploring and head out the door!

JOURNAL & SKETCH YOUR EXPERIENCE I cherish the travel journals I have kept on my trips. Some are filled with watercolor scenes of our explorations, and others are just scribbled diaries of what we did that day. For me, a travel journal is not supposed to be perfect. It's an organic document of memories and stories while in a location. There's space throughout this book to write just the facts, and room to embellish your feelings and memories of the day.

PHOTO OP
Don't miss these photo opportunities! Look for this symbol throughout the book to find nearby sights for that perfect snapshot.

GET CREATIVE This book is all about getting creative and engaging the local area you are exploring to have a unique and memorable experience. So if you have an inspiring idea, go for it! Some chapters provide artsy projects, some interactive games, while others encourage you to have fun with creative writing. The activities are meant to be spontaneous and entertaining. But you could also save the book activities until later in the day, perhaps at a cafe, or back at the hotel as you relive your adventures.

Now, it's time to get exploring!

ART SUPPLIES

I've learned over time that for packing art supplies, fewer is always better. A few black pens, a travel watercolor set, and a couple colored pencils are typically all I need. Occasionally, I'll bring along a glue stick or tape to add a unique wrapper, ticket stub, or scrap of paper I may find to my journal. You'll find plenty of room in the diary section for all these artistic and creative endeavors and any others you may think up!

THE GUIDE

PHOTO THEMES

A photo theme is a great way to see things you may not initially notice when touring a new spot. It's like a scavenger hunt to help you look beyond the sights and uncover the patterns and unique personality of a city. All you need is your phone and a theme—a color, an object, a style, an animal, etc. As you tour the city, hunt for your theme and snap a photo when you see it. By the end of the day, you may have taken ten pictures or hundreds of them.

Once you've taken all these fabulous pictures, you can make DIY souvenir gifts for yourself! Create an art collage using a multi-photo frame, or put it all together in an artsy photo book. Here are some possible photo themes you can use.

INTERNATIONAL ORANGE

The Golden Gate Bridge is not golden at all. In fact, the color is called "international orange."

While touring the city, hunt for more instances of this iconic color. It could be the color of a car, a house, a souvenir at a gift shop, a T-shirt someone is wearing, or a logo of a business. Once you keep your eyes out for this color, you'll be surprised how often you see it!

THE HILLS OF SAN FRANCISCO

San Francisco is built on hills. In fact, some are very steep! Just walk from Coit Tower down to North Beach, then over to Russian Hill. You'll quickly get a flavor for the hills of San Francisco.

Hunt for these spectacular hills and start taking pictures: from a block away, looking up the hill, looking down the hill, of cars parked at angles, or of "steep hill" signs.

PAINTED LADY PORTRAITS

Many San Francisco neighborhoods are filled with wonderful Victorian homes. Their ornate architectural detailing and elaborate colors have earned them the name "Painted Ladies."

Take full shots of single Victorian homes, or narrow your photo to just the front steps and door. You could focus on only the fanciful woodwork and details, or you could take photos of the Painted Ladies in full rows. Use any or all these ideas and capture the true personality of these historic gals.

The Painted Ladies are at Steiner Street and Hayes Street.

TRANSPORTATION

From cable cars to ferries, trolleys to buses, unicycles to bicycles, a transportation photo theme offers a unique view at how San Franciscans get around.

The iconic cable cars are a sight to see on their own but are limited to such a small portion of the city. Branch out and take a ride down the waterfront on one of the many styled trolleys (some are imported from cities around the world). Or head to the piers for a ferry ride. If you like bikes, spend time in SOMA and watch the bike messengers zip by, or take a picnic to Golden Gate Park and be entertained by a juggling unicyclist. There is no shortage of modes of transportation in San Francisco, so be sure to have your camera charged up and ready to go!

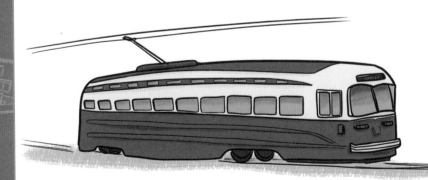

FISHERMAN'S WHARF

As gold diggers flocked to San Francisco in the mid-1800s to find riches, it became apparent that these hungry workmen needed to be fed. Many Chinese immigrants who fished for shrimp, oysters, and salmon in the bay came to their aid. Italian immigrants joined in after and set up fish stands along the beach to serve the hungry workers.

The Italian fishermen painted and named their lateen-rigged sailboats after patron saints, much as they had done back in Italy. There are tales of these men singing Italian operatic arias to each other on foggy days to communicate while fishing.

Soon, gasoline engine boats arrived (known as putt-putts), then larger commercial fishing boats which allowed for year-round fishing of a much wider area and range. Today, many fishermen find their catch by the Farallon Islands, 30 miles outside of the Golden Gate Bridge.

CRAB SEASON

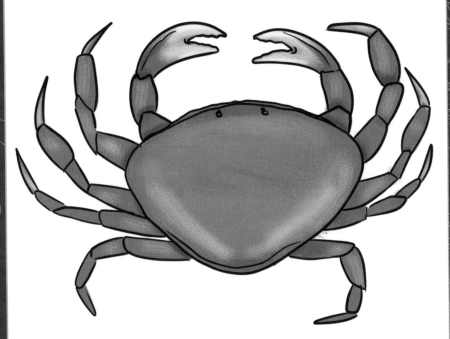

Locals eagerly await the opening of Dungeness crab season every year in November. Many San Franciscans serve a big feast of cracked Dungeness crab, melted butter, and sourdough bread during the holidays instead of the more traditional turkey or ham.

EAT CRAB AT A RESTAURANT
Eating Dungeness crab is truly a rite of passage to visiting San Francisco. Be sure to wear a bib when you indulge for the perfect selfie!

INTERVIEW A FISHERMAN

Many of the restaurants in Fisherman's Wharf today (like Alioto's and Castagnola's) still grace the names of the first-generation Italian fishermen who worked the area. With such a long history, the fishermen today surely have a story or two to tell! Spend a little time wandering along the docks of Jefferson Street and look for a fisherman (or fisherwoman) to interview to hear their tales. Use the questions below to prompt some interesting responses you won't soon forget.

What's your name?
_____

How long have you been a fisherman?
_____

Has fishing been in your family a long time?
_____
_____

What's the origin or meaning of the name of the boat you work on?
_____
_____

What makes fishing in San Francisco unique?
_____
_____

What's it like to fish in the fog?
_____
_____
_____

What's your favorite fish?

_____

_____

What's your favorite part of your job? Worst part?

_____

_____

Share one of your favorite fishing stories.

_____

_____

_____

_____

_____

_____

Bonus! Sketch a portrait of your fisherman and/or the fisherman's boat.

CIOPPINO
(THE ITALIAN FISHERMAN'S STEW)

After a hard day's work, the Italian fishermen would head home to neighboring North Beach and make a seafood stew using the leftovers from the catch of the day. This tomato-based stew is known as Cioppino and is served at many of the restaurants today along Fisherman's Wharf and throughout the city. This recipe makes approximately 6 to 8 servings.

3 tablespoons extra virgin olive oil
1½ cups diced onions
2 tablespoons chopped garlic
¼ cup tomato paste
1 cup dry white wine
2½ pounds diced tomatoes
1 red bell pepper, diced
¼ cup chopped basil
2 tablespoons chopped parsley
1 tablespoon chopped thyme
1 bay leaf
3 cups fish stock
1 cooked crab
12 to 15 clams
15 mussels
1 pound large shrimp
½ pound scallops
½ pound squid
Sourdough bread,
  for serving

In a large stock pot over medium-high heat, sauté the diced onions and chopped garlic in the olive oil. Stir in the tomato paste and then the white wine. Bring to a simmer and reduce by half.

Add the diced tomatoes, red bell pepper, basil, parsley, thyme, and bay leaf, and cook for a few minutes until blended.

Then add the fish stock and cook, covered, for 30 minutes to soak up flavors.

Add the crab, clams, mussels, shrimp, scallops, and squid to the soup, and let it simmer until everything is fully cooked and the mussels and clams have opened, about 7 to 10 minutes.

Serve in a bowl with a side of San Francisco sourdough bread.

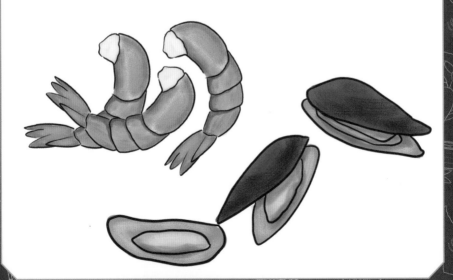

ALCATRAZ

The infamous Alcatraz was once home to America's most dangerous criminals. This rocky island in the middle of the San Francisco Bay was first discovered by Spanish explorer Juan Manuel de Ayala who named it La Isla de los Alcatraces, or Island of the Pelicans, for all the pelicans and birds that inhabited it. By the mid-1850s, President Fillmore claimed the island for the US government. The first lighthouse on the West Coast was built on it, and soon it became a military prison for the next 80 years. Actually, the prisoners held on the island had built the cellhouses, along with other buildings on the island.

UNITED STATES PENITENTIARY
ALCATRAZ ISLAND   AREA 12 ACRES
1½ MILES TO TRANSPORT DOCK
ONLY GOVERNMENT BOATS PERMITTED
OTHERS MUST KEEP OFF 200 YARDS
NO ONE ALLOWED ASHORE
WITHOUT A PASS

By the early 1930s, the US Justice Department was in desperate need of an impenetrable prison that could hold the most deplorable and difficult prisoners that other prisons across the nation just couldn't seem to control. Alas, the notorious Alcatraz as we know it was born.

WHAT'S YOUR CRIMINAL NAME?

Many of Alcatraz's famous inmates had nicknames to inspire fear: Al "Scarface" Capone, George "Machine Gun" Kelly, Alvin "Creepy Karpis" Karpowicz, James "Whitey" Bulger, and Robert "Birdman of Alcatraz" Stroud.

Use the first letter of your last name to find your criminal name, or come up with your own dastardly moniker.

A = Pistol	N = Bloody
B = Ice Pick	O = Bootlegger
C = Eliminator	P = Rat
D = Toxic	Q = Undertaker
E = Liquidator	R = Killer
F = Butcher	S = Diablo
G = Reaper	T = Mad Dog
H = Garrote	U = Deranged
I = Hatchet	V = Hangman
J = Conman	W = Automatic
K = Cleaver	X = Enforcer
L = Swindler	Y = Slayer
M = Cyanide	Z = Trigger Happy

Your First Name _____

+ Your Last Name _____

= Criminal Nickname: _____

PEEK THROUGH THE CELL BARS

Every visitor to famed Alcatraz needs to take a picture behind bars! Make sure your expression matches your crime.

WANTED!

Were you caught for high treason? Embezzlement? Murder? Espionage? Robbery? Arson? Extortion? Mobbing? Piracy? Conspiracy? In the space below, write down your alleged crime. Be as detailed as you like; after all, you are being sent to the most infamous prison in the US.

_____

_____

_____

_____

_____

_____

_____

_____

_____

_____

_____

_____

_____

_____

_____

_____

_____

ASSOCIATE WARDEN'S RECORD CARD

OFFENSE _____

SENTENCE _____

PREVIOUS RECORD _____

CRIMES INVOLVED _____

AGE _____
MARRIED _____
CITIZEN _____
PHYSICAL COND. _____
MENTAL COND. _____
PSYCHOLOGY and APTITUDE _____
OCCUPATION _____

HISTORY

OCCUPATIONS	NO. YEARS	VERIFICATION

NAME _____ NUMBER _____

ASSOCIATE WARDEN'S RECORD CARD

OFFENSE kidnapping

SENTENCE 28 years

PREVIOUS RECORD kidnapping burglary

CRIMES INVOLVED burglary

AGE 32
MARRIED no
CITIZEN US
PHYSICAL COND. average
MENTAL COND. ok
PSYCHOLOGY + APTITUDE anxiety
OCCUPATION construction

HISTORY

OCCUPATIONS	NO. YEARS	VERIFICATION
building	5	brother
shopkeeper	2	Mr. Keen

NAME Joe "the Regular" Rapone NUMBER 098...

Fill out the card above with your criminal details. Include a drawing of yourself or add a photo in the center to make it complete.

ASSOCIATE WARDEN'S RECORD CARD

OFFENSE murder

SENTENCE life without parole

PREVIOUS RECORD murder robbery

CRIMES INVOLVED burglary

AGE 28
MARRIED no
CITIZEN US
PHYSICAL COND. strong
MENTAL COND. ok
PSYCHOLOGY + APTITUDE cunning
OCCUPATION machinist

HISTORY

OCCUPATIONS	NO. YEARS	VERIFICATION
auto repair	3	Mr. Windel
home repair	2	Mr. Bates

NAME Albert "the Axe" Winters NUMBER 8860332

PLAN YOUR ESCAPE FROM ALCATRAZ

In Alcatraz's 29 years as a federal prison, there were 14 attempted escapes involving 36 prisoners. Of the 36 inmates, 23 of them were captured, 6 were shot and killed during their escape, 2 of them drowned, and 5 went missing or were presumed dead, never to be seen again.

Now it's time to plan your escape. You've been on Alcatraz for 13 years and have schemed a devious plot to break free. Use the map on the next page to draw your escape path. Make note of aids, obstacles, guards, inmates, or others you may encounter along the way.

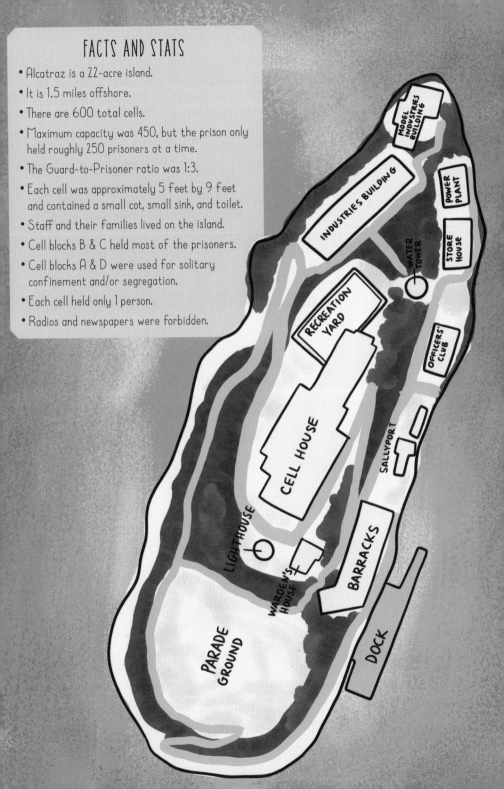

FACTS AND STATS

- Alcatraz is a 22-acre island.
- It is 1.5 miles offshore.
- There are 600 total cells.
- Maximum capacity was 450, but the prison only held roughly 250 prisoners at a time.
- The Guard-to-Prisoner ratio was 1:3.
- Each cell was approximately 5 feet by 9 feet and contained a small cot, small sink, and toilet.
- Staff and their families lived on the island.
- Cell blocks B & C held most of the prisoners.
- Cell blocks A & D were used for solitary confinement and/or segregation.
- Each cell held only 1 person.
- Radios and newspapers were forbidden.

PIER 39

Many cities across the US have bustling waterfront attractions like San Francisco's Pier 39, but what makes this spot so uniquely San Franciscan is not necessarily the pier itself but its almost year-round residents—the sea lions! In the fall of 1989, around a dozen California sea lions began to inhabit the docks along Pier 39. Before this time, most sea lions had spent their time lounging on Seal Rocks, a group of rock formations just slightly offshore in the Pacific Ocean near Lands End of the Outer Richmond District of San Francisco.

What brought the sea lions to Pier 39's docks is not entirely known, but most likely they felt more protected inside the bay. By early 1990, over 150 animals had taken up residence. Although the boat owners of that dock were quite frustrated with their new guests, news of their arrival gained media attention, and soon the sea lions became an attraction of their own.

The population over time ebbs and flows based on the season and availability of food. At one point there were 1,701 sea lion residents. The sea lions occasionally disappear from the docks altogether, most likely heading south to breed, but they always make their way back to their San Francisco home.

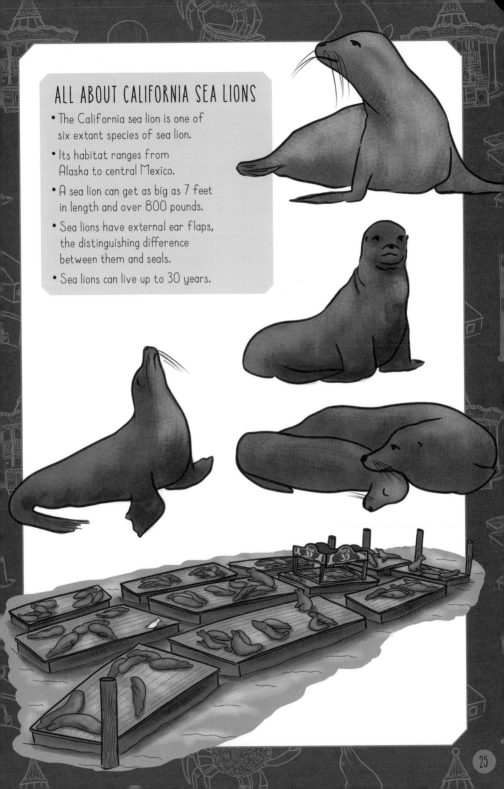

ALL ABOUT CALIFORNIA SEA LIONS

- The California sea lion is one of six extant species of sea lion.
- Its habitat ranges from Alaska to central Mexico.
- A sea lion can get as big as 7 feet in length and over 800 pounds.
- Sea lions have external ear flaps, the distinguishing difference between them and seals.
- Sea lions can live up to 30 years.

A DAY IN THE LIFE OF A SEA LION

The playful behavior and noisy barking are infectious traits of the sea lion. After shopping or dining at the pier, spend some time watching the sea lions. Use the comic panels below to create a story about the interactions you see on the docks.

NORTH BEACH

Vesuvio Cafe is at 255 Columbus Avenue.

In the mid-1800s, when North Beach was an actual beach, immigrants from around the world docked at this northernmost point in San Francisco and inhabited the area. As the decades passed, the land was filled in and populated with more fishing wharves and docks. Italian immigration soared, and by the turn of the century, Italians made up a huge portion of the community, giving the area its nickname of San Francisco's Little Italy. Wander through the neighborhood and along Grant Avenue, the oldest street in San Francisco, and you will find your share of quaint Italian restaurants, and bars and cafes to while away the afternoon. It was these same cafes and bars that attracted the Beat Generation to call North Beach its home.

THE BEATS

The streets of San Francisco,
narrow alleys next to Condor lights. Walk. Talk.
Foggy minds filled with caffeine
jungled up in narrow Victorian flats.
A cool cat jazzing on juice.
Hipsters hugging freebies.
Life lives way out and wild in San Francisco.

Jack Kerouac, Allen Ginsberg, and the rest of the beatnik gang haunted the streets of North Beach in San Francisco, in the 1950s, searching for cool sounds to play and smooth words to speak.

To get into the Beat scene, head to Vesuvio Cafe or Caffe Trieste—perfect hangout spots to watch the scene. Next, mosey over to City Lights Bookstore and thumb through their stacks of beatnik prose.

City Lights Bookstore is at 261 Columbus Avenue.

POSE ON THE STEPS OF HISTORY

Flanking one of the first parks in San Francisco, Washington Square Park, is the neo-gothic Catholic church known as the Italian Cathedral of the West, or Saints Peter and Paul Church, at 666 Filbert Street. Rebuilt after the 1906 earthquake, it has been a cultural hub for this Italian American neighborhood. It has been featured in many motion pictures throughout the years, and also has the Hollywood honor of being the steps where Marilyn Monroe and Joe DiMaggio took their wedding photos.

BEATNIK POETRY

Once you've gotten into the groove, sit down and compose your own beatnik poem. Use your experiences wandering the streets of San Francisco as fodder. Be sure to check out the glossary of beatnik terms on the next page to help with your piece. Before you know it, you'll be digging the Beat feel and swinging with the best of the hipsters.

BEATNIK SLANG

back seat bingo: *making out*

Beatsville: *a good place for Beats*

can the lip: *stop talking*

dig: *understand*

feeling hairy: *feeling good*

fuzz: *the police*

a gas: *lots of fun*

gin mill cowboy: *a regular at a bar*

a groove: *a thrilling thing to do*

jazzing: *making love*

later: *goodbye*

Nadaville: *a dull place*

noodle it out: *think it through*

red onion: *a hole-in-the-wall bar*

short trip to Rio: *a coffee break*

square or cube: *unhip person*

swinging like sixteen: *being really wild*

twin trees: *high-heeled shoes*

wigged out: *freaked out*

CAPTURE THE CORNER VIEW OF THE CITY

Views from this skinny white tower are breathtaking, or taking a photo looking up at the lit tower in the evening can be just as stunning.

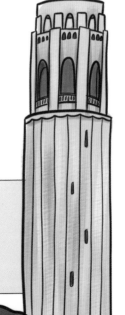

Coit Tower is at 1 Telegraph Hill Boulevard.

CHINATOWN

Chinese immigration began in earnest in the mid-1800s. In 1850 alone, approximately 25,000 immigrants came to America. Neighborhoods called "Chinatown" popped up in almost every major city in the world, but San Francisco's Chinatown remains one of the largest and oldest Chinese communities in North America, and the largest Chinatown outside of Asia. The San Francisco Planning Department has even named it "the most densely populated area west of Manhattan."

Many Chinese immigrants came to San Francisco to work in the mines during the Gold Rush, and many others took jobs as farmhands, garment workers, and laborers for the growing US railroad system. In the city, they found opportunities to serve as merchants, laundry workers, and restaurateurs. They worked hard to survive and make a new life for themselves, yet also faced an incredible amount of discrimination and hardships from not only other citizens of San Francisco but from restricting immigration laws passed by Congress. The Chinese Exclusion Act of 1882 banned Chinese immigrants from entering the country for 10 years and prohibited the Chinese from becoming naturalized citizens. The ban was finally lifted in 1943 with the passage of the Magnuson Act.

BE A MOTHER OF A DRAGON
On either side of the Dragon's Gate, at Bush Street and Grant Avenue, marking the entrance to Chinatown is a dragon statue waiting to be photographed.

The 1906 earthquake completely destroyed Chinatown. Some were eager to see that it was not rebuilt and relocated to another city entirely, but a smart businessman named Look Tin Eli quickly created a plan to rebuild Chinatown exactly where it had always been. The new neighborhood was built with the Edwardian-style architecture of the time, but Chinese-inspired decorations were added to give it the "look" of old China, yet with a more Western appeal.

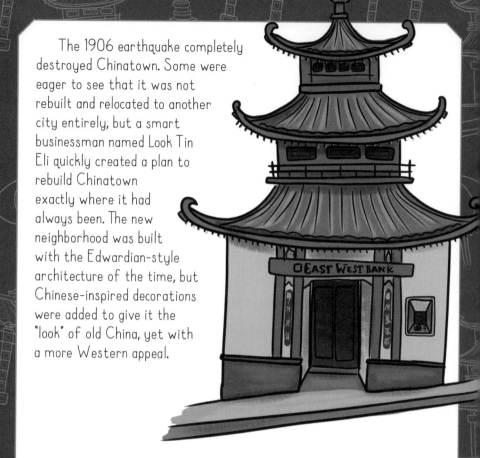

END
ROSS

HIDDEN ALLEYS

Be sure to peek down the numerous alleyways in the area, including Ross Alley, St. Louis Alley, Duncombe Alley, and Beckett Alley. Some of the rougher stories in Chinatown's history played out in these small streets in the forms of gambling, prostitution, and opium dens.

Fast forward a hundred years, Chinatown is now one of the top tourist destinations in San Francisco. Walk through the Dragon's Gate and down Grant Street, and you'll quickly feel as if you've left the city entirely! Many buildings built following the earthquake, including the Sing Fat and Sing Chong buildings at Grant and Pine, are still standing and great reminders of this long-established neighborhood.

DIMSUM

GALLERY

ALL ABOUT THE FORTUNE COOKIE

Roughly 3 billion fortune cookies are made every year. But contrary to popular belief, the fortune cookie is not from China.

The origin of the cookie has been hotly debated for years. Some believe the first type of fortune cookie originated in Japan sometime in the late 1800s. Others claim it is an American invention, but it's debatable which American created it. The contention is between two Californians—a Chinese immigrant from Los Angeles named David Jung, and a Japanese immigrant in San Francisco named Makoto Hagiwara (who is also the designer of the Japanese Tea Garden in Golden Gate Park). Both men's families claim they were the first to invent the cookie in the early 1900s.

Because Americans are very fond of something sweet at the end of a meal, the fortune cookie became the treat served at the end of the meal in Chinese restaurants across the states. As for the iconic shape, initially bakers of fortune cookies used chopsticks to bend the flat circular cookie while still hot.

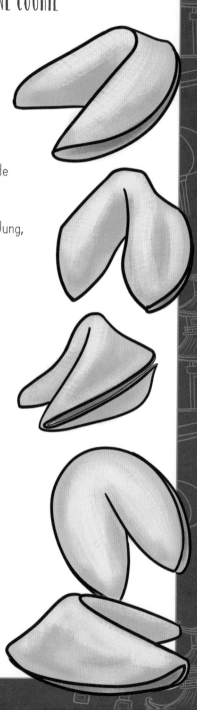

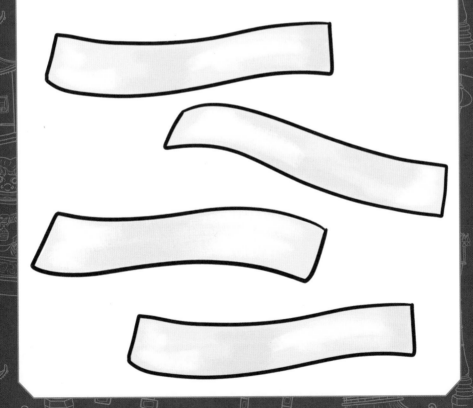

CREATE YOUR OWN FORTUNE

Give a try at writing your own fortune on the slips below. Use these writing "formulas" to help craft the perfect fortune, or make up your own formula!

FORTUNE FORMULAS

- [*Today/tomorrow/next year*] + [*prediction*] + [*contradiction*].

- [*Object of desire*] will be plentiful in your future.

- True love is [*interesting metaphor*].

- [*A daredevil act*] is exciting, but [*a less dangerous act*] is safer.

- [*Your Name*] says, [*your greatest fear*] only comes true if you believe it will happen.

FERRY BUILDING

It's hard to imagine what San Francisco must have been like without the Golden Gate and Bay Bridges. Prior to the mid-1930s, the only way to access San Francisco, unless you were coming from the peninsula, was by ferry! In fact, San Francisco's Ferry Building was the second-busiest transit hub of the time, with roughly 50,000 commuters daily traipsing through its doors.

PORT OF SAN FRANCISCO

San Francisco's Ferry Building has a long history. The building first opened in 1898, replacing the wooden Ferry House from 1875. Its Beaux-Arts style was designed by architect A. Page Brown and included the 245-foot clock tower inspired by a famous bell tower in Seville, Spain. As the demand for workers in San Francisco increased, so did the ferry commuters who lived in the North and East Bay. By the mid to late 1930s, the popularity of the Ferry Building drastically changed when both the Bay Bridge (access to the East Bay) and Golden Gate Bridge (access to the North Bay) opened. Coupled with America's love of the automobile, the need for ferries decreased significantly.

By the 1950s the building was converted into offices and fell under the shadows of the double-decker freeway built along the waterfront. This area became less than desirable as it was virtually cut off from the rest of the city. In 1989, the Loma Prieta earthquake struck, rendering the freeway unusable. With the removal of the freeway, restoration of

The Ferry Building is on the Embarcadero at Market Street.

the Ferry Building and revitalization of the entire waterfront turned what was once a blight into a tourist hub in San Francisco.

Today, the Ferry Building is a bustling public food market. The stalls are filled with local fare, from cheese to charcuterie perfect to make a picnic lunch. There are also several boutique stores, trendy sit-down restaurants, as well as a huge outdoor farmers' market held three times a week. There continues to be a ferry service to the North and East Bay, just as there was over a hundred years ago, filled with tourists and commuters who don't want to brave traffic. Some might say the restoration has re-energized the life of the building to be even grander than its days as just a ferry hub.

TAKE A FOODIE SHOT

San Francisco is a foodie-heaven. Head to the Ferry Building and browse the stands and local farmers' market to pick up a delicious bite to eat. Just make sure to take your photo before you finish your food!

CAPTURE THE SIGHTS

As you meander the Ferry Building, take out a few color pencils or pens and quickly sketch the large variety of foods, produce, flowers, and crafts you see. Your loose sketches will be a great memory of the energy and pace of your visit.

SOMA

Now filled with hipsters and techies, the South of Market (SOMA) district has had its share of ups and downs over the years. When it was first settled during the Gold Rush in the mid-1800s, it was a tent city for thousands of miners waiting to strike it rich. SOMA continued to grow with residential buildings, businesses, and some industrial areas near the waterfront. With the destruction from the 1906 earthquake and the more wealthy citizens moving across Market Street, the neighborhood fell on hard times. Residential hotels filled with working single men, seasonal laborers, seamen, and transient workers, and the area grew with more warehouses and industrial businesses.

The tech boom in the late 1990s as well as urban renewal and redevelopment projects gave the SOMA area a huge boost as loft housing became hot and live-work lofts became cool. Twenty years later, SOMA is still buzzing with many of the city's best museums, the new Transbay Terminal, and loads of world-famous tech companies.

Completed in 2018, the Salesforce Tower replaced the Transamerica Pyramid as the tallest skyscraper in the city.

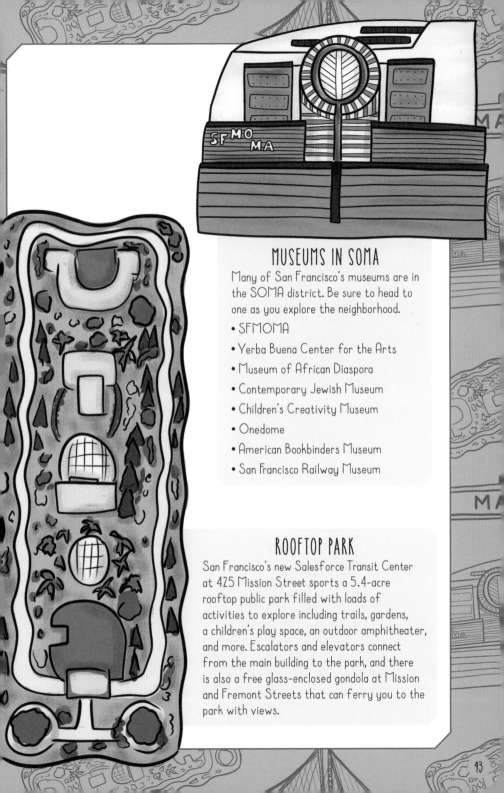

MUSEUMS IN SOMA

Many of San Francisco's museums are in the SOMA district. Be sure to head to one as you explore the neighborhood.

- SFMOMA
- Yerba Buena Center for the Arts
- Museum of African Diaspora
- Contemporary Jewish Museum
- Children's Creativity Museum
- Onedome
- American Bookbinders Museum
- San Francisco Railway Museum

ROOFTOP PARK

San Francisco's new Salesforce Transit Center at 425 Mission Street sports a 5.4-acre rooftop public park filled with loads of activities to explore including trails, gardens, a children's play space, an outdoor amphitheater, and more. Escalators and elevators connect from the main building to the park, and there is also a free glass-enclosed gondola at Mission and Fremont Streets that can ferry you to the park with views.

Wander the streets and keep your ears open. Fill the bubbles below with conversations you overhear while exploring SOMA.

THERE'S AN APP FOR THAT

Based on the conversations you overheard, brainstorm the next latest and greatest "buzzworthy" app. Grab a coffee and scribble your ideas on the napkin below.

NOB HILL

The Pacific-Union Club is at 1000 California Street.

Perched on top one of San Francisco's notorious hills, close to the heart of the city and sporting spectacular views of the Golden Gate and the Bay, is the neighborhood known as Nob Hill. The term was derived from the extremely wealthy businessmen and railroad tycoons such as Leland Stanford (the founder of Stanford University), and Collis Huntington, Mark Hopkins, and Charles Crocker, who built mansions atop the hill. They were often referred to as nabobs, which was then shortened to "nob." (Nabob is a Hindu term referring to a European who made his fortune in India or another country in the East.)

   Following closely behind the "big four" (as the men mentioned above were referred to) were mansions built by the men who profited wildly from the gold and silver bonanza, James Flood and James Flair. The very steep grade of the hill was hard to navigate, so by 1878 the California Street cable car became a reality to shuttle these wealthy tycoons to their homes. Although the names of many of these families still exist today atop Nob Hill, the 1906 earthquake and fire destroyed almost all of the mansions except for James Flood's home, which still exists today as the Pacific-Union Club.

The 1906 San Francisco earthquake was one of the world's worst natural disasters of its time. The destruction it caused and the subsequent fires that lasted for several days left an estimated 3,000* people dead and 225,000 people homeless out of a population of 400,000. Once the fires died down, over 80% of the buildings in the city had been destroyed.

*Initial reports of deaths averaged around 700 people, but an extensive research study by Gladys Hansen and Emmet Condon estimated the deaths caused directly or indirectly by the earthquake closer to 3,000 people.

1906 EARTHQUAKE FACTS

Date: Wednesday, April 18, 1906

Time: 5:12 am

Magnitude: Estimated 7.8

Fault: San Andreas

Estimated Time Length: 40 to 60 seconds

Radius Felt: From Southern Oregon to Los Angeles and as far east as Nevada

Rebuilding: Immediately following the earthquake, camps were constructed to house over 15,000 people. Donations flooded in from around the world, and plans to rebuild were quickly developed. Within roughly nine years, San Francisco had almost completely rebuilt itself in time for the 1915 Panama-Pacific International Exposition held in the city.

REPORTER ON THE SCENE

Imagine you are a young reporter with fresh eyes and a keen desire to write. You have recently moved to San Francisco, and within a month of arriving you have survived the disastrous earthquake of 1906. You can't believe the destruction and destitution you have witnessed. You've heard tales of sadness and heartbreak as well as stories of heroism and bravery.

   Your job is to report what you have seen, heard, and learned. Use your imagination and the facts listed in the box on page 47 to write what it must have been like to survive the earthquake and what you would have witnessed in the following days, weeks, and months. The world is waiting for your story.

_____

_____

_____

_____

_____

_____

_____

_____

_____

_____

_____

_____

_____

_____

HOT off the PRESS

_____

_____

_____

_____

_____

_____

_____

_____

The Call-Chronicle-Examiner

SAN FRANCISCO, THURSDAY, APRIL 19, 1906

NO HOPE LEFT FOR SAFETY OF ANY BUILDINGS | **WHOLE CITY IS ABLAZE** | **CHURCH OF SAINT IGNATIUS IS DESTROYED**

EARTHQUAKE COTTAGES

Many San Franciscans displaced by the 1906 earthquake were housed by the Army in tents and then cottages, or "earthquake shacks," in the Presidio. The tenants paid $2 a month toward eventually owning the $50 cottage. By 1908 the camps in the Presidio were closed, and the cottage owners had relocated their homes to areas around the city. Two cottages can be seen in the Presidio today at the corner of Lincoln Boulevard and Funston Avenue behind the old hospital.

THE MISSION

Mission Dolores Park
is at Dolores Street
and 19th Street.

The Mission District is the oldest inhabited neighborhood in San Francisco, having been inhabited for several thousands of years! The Yelamu tribe, part of the Ohlone people, had lived and thrived in this area, making it home for centuries. In the late 1700s the Spanish came, and in 1776 Father Francisco Palóu had a mission built named Mission San Francisco de Asís. The Spanish used the Native Americans as slave labor to build this small mission. Sadly, in just a few decades, thousands of the Ohlone people died due to disease and the conditions.

As the Spanish empire fell, Californios (Latin Americans born in Alta California, the Mexican land that is now known as California) took over the missions and turned them into ranchos. Several streets in San Francisco's Mission District are named after the rancho families of Valenciano, Guerrero, Dolores, Bernal, Noé, and de Haro.

Mission Dolores
Basilica is at
3321 16th Street.

Soon the missions/ranchos lost their status and a more decadent lifestyle with attractions such as bullfighting, horse racing, and baseball took over the Mission. Following the Gold Rush, in the mid-1800s, workers from the factories, shipyards, and restaurants took up residence here, as well as immigrants from Germany, Italy, and Ireland. Even before the earthquake of 1906, the Mission District had become a richly diverse neighborhood, much like it still is today.

Toward the second half of the twentieth century, waves of Central Americans started to arrive in the Mission, many seeking refuge from their politically unstable home countries. In the '60s urban renewal projects throughout the city and including the Mission heightened racial and class tensions. Many artists began using the walls of the neighborhood as activism to spread their message with colorful murals. Today, the Mission is filled with hundreds of murals with a wide variety of themes, including social injustice and struggles, Mayan and Aztec history, Latino history, and even everyday art with positive messages.

THE MURALS OF THE MISSION

Murals and street art can be found throughout San Francisco, but the Mission District is especially known for this colorful storytelling art. Here are some locations where you can find just a few of the murals in the neighborhood:

- **BALMY ALLEY** (between 24th and 25th; Treat and Harrison Streets) Some of the first street art in this alley is from 1971. In the 1980s many more murals were added to address the struggles and desire for peace in Central America. The alley continues to change over time, telling countless artistic stories.

- **CLARION ALLEY** (between 17th and 18th; Valencia and Mission Streets) Inspired by the works along Balmy Alley, many of the murals here are  created by the Clarion Alley Mural Project, a grassroots community organization aimed at producing artwork that supports social, economic, and political messages.

- **500 YEARS OF RESISTANCE** (on 24th and Florida Streets) Isaias Mata, a Salvadorian, painted this bright mural discussing the Spanish conquest in the New World and the aftermath.

- **WOMEN'S WISDOM THROUGH TIME**, also known as *Maestrapeace* (on The Women's Building, 18th Street between Guerrero and Valencia) Painted in 1994 by seven local muralists, this large mural is a tribute to struggles, issues, and courage of women all over the world.

- **EL ARROYO LAUNDROMAT** (on Harrison at 23rd Street) Painted by Ernesto Paul on the side of the laundromat, this mural shows a scene of women washing clothes in a rural setting (said to be the laundromat owner's hometown). Within the mural are stories of history from Colonial to Revolutionary times.

THE MISSION BURRITO

After exploring the murals throughout the Mission District, be sure to stop at a local taqueria to experience the famed "Mission burrito," a large burrito stuffed with an assortment of ingredients and wrapped in an extra-large flour tortilla. Although hotly debated, La Cumbre Taqueria is said to be creators of this filling fare. Regardless of which taqueria you end up at, the Mission burrito is a true San Francisco experience.

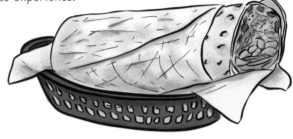

POSE BY A MURAL
Social media is filled with artsy pictures of folks alongside colorful walls. The Mission will offer a plethora of backdrops for the perfect photo with the hundreds of murals in the neighborhood.

GET INSPIRED BY THE MISSION

Make your own mark in this alley of the Mission District. Perhaps tell the story of your own heritage and history, or create a mural of a collage of the sites you explored while in San Francisco.

_____

_____

_____

_____

_____

_____

_____

_____

_____

_____

_____

_____

_____

_____

_____

_____

_____

_____

_____

_____

MEXICAN TAQUERIA

TAQU

FISH TACO $4

MISSION Burrito HERE

THE CASTRO

The Castro Theatre is at 429 Castro Street.

On the slopes of Twin Peaks is the bustling LGBTQIA+ neighborhood, the Castro. Known as Eureka Valley, this prime land was inhabited with ranchos who belonged to Mexican landowners such as José Castro and José de Jesús Noé. During the 1880s Irish, German, and Scandinavian families also settled in this area, creating a community of dairy farms and Victorian houses. When the Market Street Cable Railway extended the line to the upper Market area and Castro Street in the late 1880s, the neighborhood became accessible to other parts of San Francisco and brought more working-class families to the area to settle and build beautiful Victorians for their extended family.

Unscathed by the fires of the 1906 earthquake, the Castro remained much the same until World War II, when the US military sought out and discharged gay personnel because of their sexuality. From San Francisco's early days of the sexually charged Barbary Coast, the city had a reputation for being tolerant and liberal. Homosexuals found comfort in San Francisco after the war living in various neighborhoods throughout the city.

As families began to flee to the suburbs in the 1950s, the beautiful Victorians of the Castro became available and attracted many middle class, well-educated gay men to the area. This coincided with two other prominent social movements in San Francisco, the Beat Generation of the '50s and the hippies and Summer of Love in the '60s (see pages 29, 64–65). Both movements fueled counterculture ideas supporting the rise of gay culture by denouncing traditional middle-class American values and supporting a more open society of free love.

By the 1970s the Castro was cemented as a gay mecca. Residents were passionate about social and political justice for homosexuals and raising awareness against the many prejudices they still faced. Castro resident and civil rights activist Harvey Milk rose to political power, and in 1977 became the first openly gay elected official in California's history. His shocking assassination only a year later revealed the strong resistance the gay community still endured, yet also confirmed the community's commitment to continue to pave new paths.

By the early '80s the AIDS epidemic struck. The tragic effects of the disease and loss of so many young lives could be seen daily on the streets of the neighborhood. Activists and grassroot efforts sprang up to push local, regional, and national governments and the medical community to act and find answers and treatments. San Francisco's effort on these fronts guided many communities and governments around the world to help fight the disease.

Today, the Castro is not only a thriving, safe neighborhood for the LGTBQIA+ community, but also a popular tourist destination in San Francisco that should not be missed.

TWIN PEAKS TAVERN

For bars and taverns across the country, installing glass windows onto the street would not bring many to bat an eye, but when same-sex couple

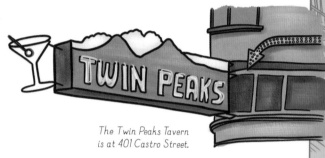

The Twin Peaks Tavern is at 401 Castro Street.

Mary Ellen Cunha and Peggy Forster did this in the early 1970s to the Twin Peaks Tavern they owned, it was a significant deal. Their tavern became the first gay bar "open" for the public to see. In 2013 the Twin Peaks Tavern became an official historic San Francisco landmark.

RAINBOW HONOR WALK

Keith Haring
(1958 - 1990)
American artist and social activist whose distinctive outline figures express universal concepts of birth, sex, love and joy

Keith Haring

Take a walk on the Rainbow Honor Walk along Castro Street, between 18th Street and Market Street, and get a history lesson of notable LGBTQ individuals who made significant contributions to the world in their field, from historic artists and writers such as Frida Kahlo, Keith Haring, Allen Ginsberg, and Gertrude Stein, to mathematician Alan Turing and astronaut Sally Ride.

SHOW YOUR PRIDE

Social and political activism has been a cornerstone of the Castro for many decades. Gay activist and artist Gilbert Baker created the Rainbow Flag in response for the need for a symbol that represents LGBTQ pride and social movements. With this activist spirit in mind, decorate the signs and banners of this parade scene below with your views.

JAPANTOWN

Nihonmachi blooms
Tea houses, ramen, gifts, sweets
A peace pagoda

Japanese immigrants came to San Francisco in the early 1860s and settled in Chinatown and South Park in SOMA. When the 1906 earthquake destroyed those neighborhoods, they moved out beyond the fire break to the Western Addition neighborhood and created a roughly 30-block enclave called Nihonjin Machi, or Japanese People's Town.

The immigrants prospered, building homes and businesses that soon became one of the largest Japanese communities outside of Japan. When WWII broke out and after the bombing of Pearl Harbor, roughly 5,000 San Franciscans of Japanese ancestry were sent to internment camps with the authorization of Executive Order 9066. With their neighborhood vacant, an influx of African Americans from the South came to live in this neighborhood and the surrounding Fillmore District to work for the war industries and the shipyards.

The Japantown Peace Plaza and the Peace Pagoda are at Post Street and Buchanan Street.

After the war, few Japanese chose to return to San Francisco as many relocated to other cities, suburbs, or different states. Regardless of the smaller population, the others moved back to their old neighborhood to rebuild their lives. Urban renewal in the 1960s built the more modern Japantown (renamed Nihonmachi) that we see today. It encompasses a six-square block radius consisting of three large malls (Miyako, the East Mall; Kintetsu, the West Mall; and Kinokuniya Mall), an outdoor pedestrian street, and the Peace Plaza, with a five-story pagoda, a gift from the city of Osaka.

Today, Japantown buzzes with many cultural attractions including delicious Japanese cuisine, gifts, bathhouses, and the popular Cherry Blossom Festival in April.

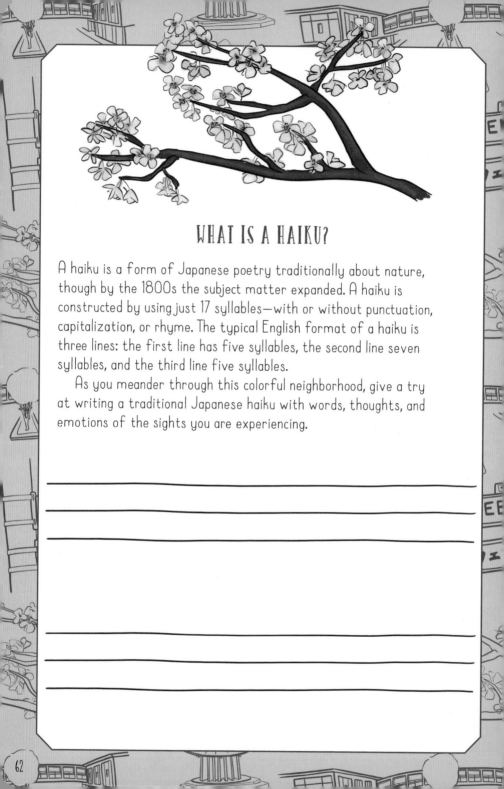

WHAT IS A HAIKU?

A haiku is a form of Japanese poetry traditionally about nature, though by the 1800s the subject matter expanded. A haiku is constructed by using just 17 syllables—with or without punctuation, capitalization, or rhyme. The typical English format of a haiku is three lines: the first line has five syllables, the second line seven syllables, and the third line five syllables.

As you meander through this colorful neighborhood, give a try at writing a traditional Japanese haiku with words, thoughts, and emotions of the sights you are experiencing.

HAIGHT-ASHBURY

In 1967 over 100,000 young, free-minded hippies converged on San Francisco's Haight-Ashbury neighborhood. It started in January when a "Human Be-In" was held in Golden Gate Park, adjacent to the Haight. Timothy Leary, American psychologist and LSD advocate, spoke to the crowd and said the famous line, "Turn on, tune in, drop out!" By spring break of that year, even more high school and college-aged kids flooded the area.

    City officials were not happy with this influx of free-loving people, yet their efforts to discourage them from coming backfired. The press and news articles written about the scene inadvertently enticed thousands of more hippies to descend on the Haight.

In a few months, the Summer of Love was in full swing. Music of the Grateful Dead, Jefferson Airplane, Jimi Hendrix, Janis Joplin, The Mamas and the Papas, and The Who, along with experimental hallucinogenic drugs, fueled the scene for an epic experience. Yet, as fast as the hippies arrived, by October of that year most had all left, returning to school, getting a job, or just moving on to another experience.

The Haight to this day still retains much of this hippie vibe. Many cafes and restaurants have an organic, worldly spin. Stores burst with tie-dye ware and peace-loving goods. Smoke shops stock an array of paraphernalia. Even the Victorian homes that surround the neighborhood stand out to be just as colorful as their inhabitants.

THE HIPPIE MOVEMENT OF THE '60S

Stemming from the previous Beat Generation, many young (and some older) folks were looking for a life where traditional societal conventions did not exist. Some were politically motivated, leery of the government and active protestors of the Vietnam War. Others were against consumerism and rigid societal norms stemming from the post-WWII era.

They explored Eastern spiritual practices; embraced music, poetry, and art; and used psychedelic drugs like LSD and mushrooms to "free their minds." They yearned for love, communal living, and freedom of expression as they searched for a deeper meaning to their existence.

MAKE YOUR OWN TIE-DYE T-SHIRT

Although the process of tie-dying fabrics and clothing has been done in cultures around the world, it is most commonly associated with the hippie movement of the '60s. After wandering the Haight, grab a coffee and some colored pencils and get creative decorating your own tie-dye shirt.

HIPPIE HILL

One popular spot in the '60s to hang out was Hippie Hill in Golden Gate Park, just a few blocks from Haight-Ashbury. This grassy knoll remains a lively scene to this day. Folks can be seen enjoying a rhythmic drum circle, strumming guitars, and lounging in the sun. It's the perfect spot to settle down and people-watch while you color your tie-dye shirt.

CREATE SOCIAL JUSTICE BUTTONS

Soon after the pin-backed button was invented at the turn of the century, the popularity of buttons stating varied political positions and announcing causes grew. During the '60s and '70s protest buttons were a key part of the hippie movement. Use the circles below to create your own buttons stating your views on social justice issues today.

HANG OUT BENEATH THE LADY'S LEGS

It's hard to miss the oversized legs hanging out of a second-story window on funky Haight Street, between Masonic Avenue and Ashbury Street. They will undoubtedly make a memorable photo.

GOLDEN GATE PARK

The Conservatory of Flowers is at 100 JFK Drive.

By the second half of the 1800s, when San Francisco had established itself as a bona fide city, urban planners decided it was time to dedicate land for public recreation and create an urban park, much like New York City had done with Central Park in 1858. The city worked with famed landscape architect Frederick Olmsted (co-designer of Central Park) who proposed a plan of a broad promenade crossing the city with parks interspersed along the way. He claimed this proposal would be better suited for San Francisco's drier climate than a large, forested park similar to New York City.

FLY DOWN A SLIDE ON A CARDBOARD MAT

The concrete chutes at the Koret Children's Quarter are a San Francisco classic! Grab a piece of cardboard to sit on, and whiz down the slide for the perfect action shot.

The city dismissed the plan and acquired land in the western portion of the city known as the Great Sand Waste, a part of the Outside Lands. The windswept dunes seemed an unlikely area for a lush park setting, yet William Hammond Hall, the new engineer assigned to design the park, persisted in finding vegetation and trees that would take root and flourish. The park was also designed with many attractions suited for all the people of the city to enjoy (a relatively new concept in city planning at the time, again spearheaded by Olmsted, that essentially defines the idea of a public park to this day).

Today, you will find many of Hall's original attractions still exist, and many more have been added. Golden Gate Park is a nature lover's paradise including a myriad of pathways, lakes, well-tended gardens, animals, and diverse scenery for hours, if not days, to explore!

The Dutch Windmill is one of two historic windmills in the western section of the park.

69

THINGS TO SEE & DO IN GOLDEN GATE PARK

GOLDEN GATE PARK

- ☐ Rent a paddle boat and explore Stow Lake and Huntington Falls.
- ☐ Ride on a vintage carousel near Koret Children's Quarter.
- ☐ See tulips and the famous Dutch and Murphy Windmills.
- ☐ Visit the de Young Museum and get a spectacular view at the Hamon Observation Tower.
- ☐ Take up lawn bowling.
- ☐ Join the Angling & Casting Club and perfect your fishing skills.
- ☐ Play 9 holes at the Golden Gate Park Golf Course.
- ☐ Gaze at Uncle John's Tree, named for the park's superintendent John McLaren and planted in the 1880s.
- ☐ Catch an outdoor concert at the polo fields.
- ☐ Watch bison roam around their paddock.

- ☐ Watch locals boogie on roller skates at 6th Avenue Skate Park.
- ☐ Run some laps around Kezar Stadium.
- ☐ Learn about rare and unusual plants at the Conservatory of Flowers.
- ☐ Travel back in time and imagine life in the 1911 Pioneer Log Cabin.
- ☐ Throw horseshoes with friends at the pits.
- ☐ Dance to the drum circle at Hippie Hill.
- ☐ Bike for miles along the winding pathways in the park.
- ☐ Head to an underwater world at Steinhart Aquarium in the California Academy of Sciences.
- ☐ Grab a racket and play a set of tennis.
- ☐ Stop and smell the roses at the Rose Garden.
- ☐ Recite poetry at the Shakespeare Garden.
- ☐ Enroll in an art class at the Sharon Building.
- ☐ Take pause at the AIDS Memorial Grove.
- ☐ Listen to music at the Music Concourse bandshell.
- ☐ Discover a world of plants at the San Francisco Botanical Garden.

SING ON STAGE

Join past performer greats such as the Grateful Dead and Luciano Pavarotti and make your stage debut under the Music Concourse bandshell at Golden Gate Park.

NATURE WALK

Take a nature walk in Golden Gate Park and use the prompts below to experience the beauty around you.

Color this square to capture the color palette of your walk.

Whether it's a bug or a large bison, make a quick sketch of the animals you see on your walk.

Make a collage with fallen flower petals.

Create simple doodles of flowers you see.

Get super close to a flower or leaf and sketch the micro details.

Capture a silhouette of the landscape you see in front of you.

Bonus! Take time on your nature walk to leave a little creative expression behind for others to enjoy. You could arrange a spiral design out of pebbles on the ground or stack a small pebble tower in the spirit of the art of stone balancing for people to ponder. Perhaps arrange a group of colorful leaves to create a rainbow. Passersby will love the displays of creativity with your natural public art.

JAPANESE TEA GARDEN

The Japanese Tea Garden is located at 75 Hagiwara Tea Garden Drive.

The Japanese Tea Garden in Golden Gate Park was originally created as an exhibit for the 1894 California Midwinter International Exposition. After the fair, landscape architect Makoto Hagiwara was given permission to maintain the exhibit as a permanent Japanese-style garden. He and his family lived on the grounds and expanded the garden from one to five acres. He built on the initial design to make the perfect Japanese Garden, and after his death in 1925 his daughter and her children became the proprietors and continued the maintenance of the garden. In 1942, the family was forced by the government to evacuate and move into an internment camp. Unfortunately, they were not allowed to return to their home at the garden after the war, but the tea garden was preserved and has become one of the most popular spots to visit in Golden Gate Park. This garden is also the oldest public Japanese Garden in the nation.

WALK ON THE MOON

The Drum (or Moon) Bridge reflects on still water as a circle, or the moon. Snap a moon shot, then walk across the bridge for a different perspective.

HIGHLIGHTS OF THE JAPANESE TEA GARDEN

- Tea house
- Drum (or Moon) Bridge
- Pagodas
- Stone lanterns
- Stepping stone paths
- Native Japanese plants
- Koi pond
- Zen garden

SCAVENGER HUNT

What makes San Francisco so spectacular is that it is surrounded by water on three sides. The endless Pacific Ocean crashes its waves onto Ocean Beach, which spans almost the entire western edge of the city. To the north and east is the picturesque San Francisco Bay, filled with regattas of sailboats, dotted with a few islands, and spanned by one of the world's most famous bridge, the iconic Golden Gate Bridge.

Below is a scavenger hunt to get you to explore all that San Francisco's waterfront has to offer! With your keen sleuthing skills, start with the first clue, and see where it leads. By the end of your hunt, you will be rewarded with knowing exactly why San Francisco earned the moniker City by the Bay. (Find the answers on page 111.)

CLUE 1 Nicknamed for a famed San Francisco Giants first baseman, this location is filled with kayaks, canoes, and boats waiting to catch a fly ball!

CLUE 2 Made by an artist who loves to create objects larger than life, this spot will undoubtedly inspire the romantic in us all.

CLUE 3 Facing the city some 245 feet below and having survived the massive 1906 and 1989 earthquakes, this site stands the test of time.

CLUE 4 Immerse yourself in San Francisco's notorious fog along this pedestrian bridge to understand why the quote "The coldest winter I ever saw was the summer I spent in San Francisco" is so true.

CLUE 5 To find this destination, prepare to climb. In between discovering gardens and hidden homes, be sure to turn around to soak in the stunning San Francisco Bay views.

CLUE 6 From the depths of the ocean emerges our next spot. This veteran, named after a fish, earned six battle stars, trained reservists, and has even appeared on the big screen. She's now open and ready for autographs.

CLUE 7 Grab a shovel and pail, your rod and reel, or your suit and goggles, and head to this National Historic Landmark for more stunning views of the Bay, in or out of the water.

CLUE 8 Head to this place at high tide and become entranced by the sounds of nature.

CLUE 9 Your next stop was once marshland. Infill from the 1906 earthquake then converted the area into a world showcase exposition that was torn down almost as soon as it was built. Some 100 years later, it is one of the best places to fly a kite in all of San Francisco.

CLUE 10 Come here to learn all about the life and history of this famed mouse-loving man whose stories, innovations, and legacies are world renowned.

CLUE 11 Powerful you have become in figuring out these clues, yet patience you must have to finish the hunt. Find me at this next site and feel the force!

CLUE 12 Home to 30,000 residents with honorable pasts, these hallowed grounds offer spectacular views of the Bay many defended.

CLUE 13 Get up close and personal with the underpinnings of an iconic San Francisco landmark while learning how the Bay was protected from hostiles at this historic point.

CLUE 14 Great Scott! This area not only boasts million-dollar views but is home to several key spots that kept San Francisco safe from harm for many years.

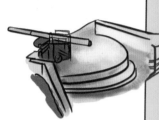

CLUE 15 Come here for an insane workout yet stay for the incredible Golden Gate view. And if you happen to visit on a warm day, you may see that for some, clothing is optional!

CLUE 16 Participate in a mindful exercise at this tranquil spot and ponder the fact that the closest land west of here is Japan.

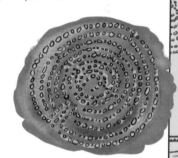

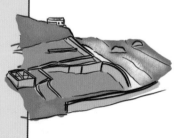

CLUE 17 Close your eyes, don your bathing cap, and imagine swimming in what was once the largest indoor pool in the world. What remains at this location may not look like much, but in a previous era it was all the rage.

CLUE 18 Built in the mid-twentieth century, this attraction may seem like magic, but it's actually the only place in San Francisco where you can see a panoramic image without a camera!

CLUE 19 On a sunny day, you may think this is paradise, but the lack of high-rises and notorious fog keeps this San Francisco secret safe from overcrowding. It's the perfect place to watch intrepid surfers ride in on waves and large cargo ships head off to Asia.

CLUE 20 Glide over to your last stop on your City by the Bay tour, where dogs run free and locals get their outdoorsy fix with numerous hiking trails, horseback riding, and lots of hang gliding.

SAN FRANCISCO NICKNAMES

Being a world-renowned city means San Francisco has earned many nicknames in its past, yet as locals will reveal, there are only a few that are acceptable! Below is a quick summary to help you fit in to the local vibe.

ACCEPTABLE NICKNAMES
- The City
- The City by the Bay
- SF

UNACCEPTABLE NICKNAMES
- Frisco
- San Fran

THE JOURNAL

BEST OF SAN FRANCISCO

Fill out the lists below with your favorites from exploring San Francisco.

BEST SIGHTS

_____
_____
_____
_____
_____
_____
_____
_____

BEST EATS

_____
_____
_____
_____
_____
_____
_____
_____

BEST SHOPPING

_____
_____
_____
_____
_____
_____
_____
_____

BEST DRINKS & NIGHTLIFE

_____
_____
_____
_____
_____
_____
_____
_____

BEST PARKS

_____
_____
_____
_____
_____
_____
_____
_____
_____
_____
_____

BEST MUSEUMS

_____
_____
_____
_____
_____
_____
_____
_____
_____

DAY

#_____

DATE _____

RATING ☆☆☆☆☆

WEATHER

PLACES VISITED

_____
_____
_____
_____
_____
_____
_____
_____

BEST EATS OF THE DAY

_____
_____
_____
_____
_____
_____

QUOTE OF THE DAY

_____
_____
_____
_____

ONLY IN SF

_____
_____
_____
_____

SOMETHING I SAW TODAY

DAY

\# _____

DATE _____   RATING ☆☆☆☆☆

WEATHER

PLACES VISITED

_____
_____
_____
_____
_____
_____
_____
_____
_____

BEST EATS OF THE DAY

_____
_____
_____
_____
_____
_____
_____
_____

❝❞ QUOTE OF THE DAY

_____
_____
_____
_____

 ## ONLY IN SF

_____
_____
_____

SOMETHING I SAW TODAY

DAY
____

DATE _____

RATING ☆☆☆☆☆

WEATHER

PLACES VISITED

_____
_____
_____
_____
_____
_____
_____
_____

BEST EATS OF THE DAY

_____
_____
_____
_____
_____
_____
_____

QUOTE OF THE DAY

_____
_____
_____

 ONLY IN SF

_____
_____
_____

SOMETHING I SAW TODAY

DAY

#____

DATE _____   RATING ☆☆☆☆☆

WEATHER

PLACES VISITED

_____
_____
_____
_____
_____
_____
_____
_____

BEST EATS OF THE DAY

_____
_____
_____
_____
_____
_____
_____
_____

QUOTE OF THE DAY

_____
_____
_____
_____

ONLY IN SF

_____
_____
_____
_____

SOMETHING I SAW TODAY

 **DAY #____**

DATE _____   RATING ☆☆☆☆☆

WEATHER

 PLACES VISITED

_____
_____
_____
_____
_____
_____
_____
_____
_____
_____

BEST EATS OF THE DAY

_____
_____
_____
_____
_____
_____
_____

QUOTE OF THE DAY

_____
_____
_____
_____

ONLY IN SF

_____
_____
_____
_____

SOMETHING I SAW TODAY

DAY

____

DATE _____

RATING ☆☆☆☆☆

WEATHER

 PLACES VISITED

_____
_____
_____
_____
_____
_____
_____
_____
_____

BEST EATS OF THE DAY

_____
_____
_____
_____
_____
_____

 QUOTE OF THE DAY

_____
_____
_____
_____

 ONLY IN SF

_____
_____
_____

SOMETHING I SAW TODAY

 **DAY #____**

DATE _____

RATING  ☆☆☆☆☆

WEATHER

PLACES VISITED

_____
_____
_____
_____
_____
_____
_____
_____
_____
_____

BEST EATS OF THE DAY

_____
_____
_____
_____
_____
_____
_____
_____

QUOTE OF THE DAY

_____
_____
_____
_____

 ## ONLY IN SF

_____
_____
_____
_____

SOMETHING I SAW TODAY

_____

_____

_____

_____

_____

_____

_____

_____

_____

_____

_____

_____

_____

SIT ON A
MOSAIC GARDEN

The 16th Avenue Tiled Steps is a Golden Gate Heights neighborhood collaboration project that has become so popular that it's a stop for many tour buses. The steps have a sea-to-sky theme that will offer many perfect staircase shots though, so they're well worth the visit. Find them on 16th Avenue at Moraga Street.

EAT A CHOCOLATE SUNDAE

With over 150 years in the chocolate business, a sundae at Ghirardelli Square is not to be missed. Snap a pic indulging in one of their delicious sundaes, or under the Ghirardelli name in lights at Ghirardelli Ice Cream & Chocolate, 900 North Point.

MEET KARL THE FOG

The microclimates in San Francisco can be quite an experience to behold as a tourist. One moment you may be basking in the sun at Union Square, and the next you are freezing in the blowing fog at Golden Gate Park. A trip to San Francisco is not complete without at least one selfie in the fog.

(ruled writing lines)

WALK THE HIDDEN PATH
Find Macondray Lane on Jones Street between Union and Green Streets. Tucked away are gardens and quaint homes waiting to be discovered along this charming pedestrian-only lane on Russian Hill.

ZIGZAG ON THE ROAD
Look up (or down)
a crooked street on
Lombard Street at
Hyde Street. Lombard
Street, dubbed the
"Crookedest street in
the World," offers loads
of opportunity for
playful photographs.

TAKE A STROLL BY THE PALACE

Originally built for the 1915 Panama-Pacific Exposition, the Palace of Fine Arts is an ornate Beaux-Arts structure and promenade just waiting to be photographed. From the detailed carvings to the majestic arches, there are plenty of places to get the perfect selfie. Find it at 3301 Lyon Street.

SEE TWIN PEAKS

Hands down, Twin Peaks, at
501 Twin Peaks Boulevard, offers
the best view in all of
San Francisco. The second tallest
peak in the city provides a
panoramic view from the Bay
to the Pacific Ocean. The peaks
actually have their own names
too—the north one is Eureka
and the south is Noe.

_____
_____
_____
_____
_____
_____
_____
_____
_____
_____

SCAVENGER HUNT ANSWERS

Clue 1: McCovey Cove, 24 Willie Mays Plaza

Clue 2: Cupid's Span at Rincon Park,
The Embarcadero & Folsom Street

Clue 3: Ferry Building, The Embarcadero &
Market Street

Clue 4: The Fog Bridge, Exploratorium, between
Pier 15 & Pier 17, The Embarcadero &
Green Street

Clue 5: Filbert Street Steps, 281 Filbert Street
at Sansome Street

Clue 6: USS *Pampanito*, Pier 45, The
Embarcadero at Fisherman's Wharf

Clue 7: Aquatic Park Pier & The Dolphin Club,
end of Van Ness Avenue

Clue 8: The Wave Organ, end of Yacht Road,
past the parking lot and yacht club
at the end of the jetty

Clue 9: Marina Green, Marina Boulevard at
Fillmore Street

Clue 10: Walt Disney Museum, 104 Montgomery
Street in The Presidio

Clue 11: Yoda Fountain, 1 Letterman Drive

Clue 12: San Francisco National Cemetery,
1 Lincoln Boulevard

Clue 13: Fort Point National Historic Site,
end of Marine Drive

Clue 14: Fort Scott and the Artillery Batteries
Cranston, Marcus-Miller, Boutelle, and
Godfrey-Langdon Court off of Lincoln
Boulevard

Clue 15: Sand Ladder at Baker Beach, trail
entrance at Lincoln Boulevard before
Pershing Drive

Clue 16: Lands End Labyrinth, Lands End Trail

Clue 17: Sutro Baths, 1004 Point Lobos Avenue

Clue 18: Camera Obscura, 1096 Point Lobos
Avenue

Clue 19: Ocean Beach, The Great Highway

Clue 20: Fort Funston, Fort Funston Road

DEDICATION

To my partner in wanderlust adventures, Frank. Whether it's a crazy train trip in Morocco, torrential rains in Prague, savoring ice cream in a tiny town in Iowa, or navigating the Tokyo subway, I am lucky to be able to explore this wonderful world with you!

Auguste Rodin's The Thinker is at the Legion of Honor at 100 34th Street.

Library of Congress Cataloging-in-Publication Data is on file

ISBN: 9781513262994

Proudly distributed by Ingram Publisher Services

Printed in China
1 2 3 4 5

Published by West Margin Press

WEST
MARGIN
PRESS

WestMarginPress.com

WEST MARGIN PRESS
Publishing Director: Jennifer Newens
Marketing Manager: Angela Zbornik
Editor: Olivia Ngai
Design & Production: Rachel Lopez Metzger